CORPORATE KARATE:

'MARTIAL ARTS IN BUSINESS SUITS'

ANGELINA A. MICHAIL

SUMMARY

This book addresses what your academic education or business school textbooks won't: the always obscure and implicit rules of the corporate game.

Successfully overcoming the challenges of corporate life requires a skillset that no one is neither formally, nor fully trained for.

And as corporate life becomes every day more complicated, your skills or perspective may not be relevant anymore.

Operating in a global economy, corporate ecosystems become more complex and matrix. Workplace becomes digital and remote and for the first time we have cases of co-existence of 5 generations in the workplace that are very different with each other.

Regardless of your position in the corporate hierarchy or your tenure in an organization the unspoken rules of the game will always require your attention and respect.

Based on real experiences from the frontline of the corporate world, this book serves as a quick and compact guide that will help you to succeed in your current working environment.

NOTE FROM THE AUTHOR

It's our experiences in life that shape us and create great stories and learnings.

The first time I started reflecting on my experiences from the corporate world, collecting examples and turning them into stories with meaningful learnings, was when I started teaching an HRM undergrad class. Young business school students hungry to know what the corporate reality is like, made me question if we are really preparing them with what it takes to succeed.

Personally, back from the days of being a young, aspiring HR executive up to my current position as Head of HR and Board Member of a multinational, I found value in knowledge coming from experience.

Inspiration for this book came exactly like that. From experiencing a what is known as "below the belt" hit in combat terminology, from an unforeseen opponent in a what started as a normal "business meeting". Although I did manage to handle the "hit" successfully and "strike back", I decided that there's never a business as usual discussion that can't go wrong and you always have to be prepared for the unexpected.

Exiting the meeting room, I took off my business suit jacket and stretched my neck to relieve the tension I felt from the previous attack. I could relate with the sensation you feel after any kind of competition game has finished (- for any type of sports lovers this feeling would be easy to relate with).

At exactly that moment the title of the book you're just reading was born:

"Corporate Karate: martial arts in business suits".

And then I smiled, channeling the rush into book writing creativity!

Conceptualizing all the distilled everyday wisdom from the corporate game into an informal "navigation system" is what you are holding in your hands.

TABLE OF CONTENTS

CHAPTER 1: PROLOGUE

Every organization, from small businesses to large corporations, has a culture. It's referred formally as organizational culture or company culture. Components of organizational culture are the values, beliefs (stated & unstated), norms and behavior of the people working within an organization.

Closely knit with the culture of an organization come organizational politics (also known as office politics or corporate game). Politics are the meaning that the employees of an organization attach to their actions and beliefs described as culture above. So, a set of dynamics between people in the workplace that can take different balance points therefore creating advantages or disadvantages for those at opposite ends of the equation.

All businesses are defined by their company culture, which in reality often portrays the internal political game that lies with the company. Some form of manipulation is usually at the center of organizational politics and thus it is typically referenced in a negative light.

Even though the corporate game is often expressed as negative I have learned, over the years, that choosing not to play the game or being ignorant to its existence can actually cause more damage than playing the game.

If you are in any type of employment, workplace politics are inherent. Regardless if you are conscious of it or not, once you are part of the corporate workplace, you are already playing the corporate game. In other words, you are already in a game of 'Corporate Karate' without even realizing it.

The goal of being aware and evaluating office politics is not so that you feed into this system by directly participating, but so that you can understand and avoid its pitfalls. Many workers and even leaders play the corporate game with the goal to form alliances, manipulate and take credit. With that in mind, can you really afford to ignore office politics? Can you imagine what happens if you decide not to play the game, while everyone else does? Playing the game becomes an automatic survival mechanism.

CHAPTER 2: RULES OF THE GAME

Just like any other game, playing the corporate game is all really about *how* you play it.

To be at the top of your game, you need to abide the rules. Similarly, to the rules in sports, the corporate game has its own rules that you must master and principles that cannot be ignored.

First, you must identify and be ready to accept the rules of the game as they are. Then learn how to navigate through office politics in the workplace using the rules to play the game correctly and with the best of your ability.

If you are competent enough you might actually be able to influence the game and bring some change to its rules, but first and foremost you have to accept the situation you find in an organization as is and integrate smoothly within it. Differently you will appear quickly to everyone as a mismatch or not good fit.

Karate is a great analogy to the corporate game in its basic principles.

Karate; Noun
An oriental system of unarmed combat using the hands and feet to deliver blows and blocks, widely practiced as a sport.

You bow when you enter, you fight based on your skillset, not weaponry and then you bow again when you exit a karate class. The reason for bowing in karate class is to show respect to your fellow students and more importantly, to your Sensei (teacher).

In a karate class there are clearly set rules around the respectful start and finish, aka bowing: respecting the rules of the game.

THE RESPECTFUL START:

Sequence to bowing is lower belt first and then the higher belt bows, as in, if you were a yellow belt, and you had to bow to a higher belt, you would bow first. It is a mark of respect that you must show to your superiors in karate. It is the same in a corporate company environment as there is a hierarchy involved and you must recognize and respect this hierarchy before you consider any kind of approach.

Understanding your position in the hierarchy, obligations, privileges and limitations that come with it is a key concept and actually vital for your longevity in an organization. Respecting the guidelines and power of your superiors as well as ensuring you never overshadow them is a dogma that applies foremost to your direct line manager as well as other senior people in hierarchy you collaborate with or work for.

Organizations are complex eco-systems. No matter how flat, non-hierarchical or matrix the organization you work for is, you cannot act as an independent agent or disrespect others in the workplace. Even if you believe you know better and are entitled to your professional opinion, you cannot act independently without considering the environment you operate in. The chain of command and reporting lines are among fundamental operating principles for an organization.

This might come easier or more difficult to you based on personality, age and experience.

However, no matter if you are the CFO of a Group of Companies or the junior accountant in a small accounting office, if you decide that you alone know better and decide to operate as an independent agent who does not respect or collaborate with others, then you will become an outsider. When that happens, it can end in an irreparable disaster for you. And by that, I mean, that you are shown to the exit door.

With a respectful start, you are entering the game predisposing your opponent in a good or bad way, which depends on the level of respect that you show your opponent. Similarly, to the karate game, when confronting others in the corporate game you must follow the rules of a respectful start as it is basic office politics to respect your co-workers, and by doing so, you will receive your respect because you are respecting the rules of the game and demonstrating by your actions that you are knowledgeable about how to interact in a respectful manner.

SMILING FACE TIGER: BE SINCERE

When you bow, you must do it properly with respect by showing that you mean it. The reason is that, if you mean it, everyone will understand that your respect is legitimate and will reciprocate with showing you the same courtesy of respect by returning the bow.

Nobody likes a two-faced individual who always has a hidden agenda. And if you are not genuine it will sooner or later show no matter the how competent you are in keeping pretenses.

It's a concept akin to the popular Chinese expression "smiling face tiger" (笑面虎).

"Smiling Face Tiger" (笑面虎);
Popular Chinese expression
The phrase is often used to refer to a person who superficially appears nice, but actually is not at and always has ulterior motives for his actions or words.

Once you are exposed it will be almost impossible to turn around the impressions formed about you and you will have a reputation that will precede you in every move in your organization.

This can quite easily happen as true intentions can never stay hidden for long. Eventually, others within your department or wider organization will read your actions and when they do, you will be classified as the office sham that they no longer entertain.

Usually people who use those means to an end are empty of any other real skillset that could bring results effectively for them. These means will become obsolete sooner or later within a company setting.

A lot depends on the type of organizational culture in each company.

However, let's say your manager or co-workers to whom you have been pretentiously respectful and managed to manipulate (using whatever means), are substituted or you are transferred in another department and the new boss does not take the same level of 'cajoling.' Where does that leave you? The best-case scenario it leaves you alone with your new manager and co-workers on the opposite side. As we said nobody likes a "smiling tiger".

THE SENSEI & THE CLASS: YOUR MANAGER & YOUR PEERS

The idea of respect to hierarchy is pretty straightforward for most people, and therefore most focus on "managing" their manager.

However, there is another group you have to address your attention to in an organization. And that is your peers.

Your peer group can be as important as your reporting lines in a company. They are the people that will make or break your reputation or might influence how your manager or other co-workers perceive you. That is why you must concentrate on how you perform in all aspects of a workplace environment and give the correct form of respects not only to the hierarchy within the company, but to your fellow co-workers on all levels. When you do this, it shows that you recognize the rules and that you play the game with respect. It also creates options for you to exit with a respectful finish when the game has to come to an end.

THE RESPECTFUL FINISH: HOW & WHEN TO QUIT THE GAME

Be prepared to finish exactly *how* you started; with the respect and commitment to the rules of the game. If you are prepared to give the respect that the company's hierarchy deserves when you first start out in the company, then be prepared to receive the benefits of the company's respect in the finish line of the game.

By your proper conduct during the game you should have created options for a graceful exit. Playing by the rules provides assurance for a good exit treatment to you by the organization and a path to a possible respectful return or simply good referrals.

The corporate game might be over for you in the organization you are exiting from, but unless you are leaving with pension, chances are you are just changing companies and entering a new game. Having endorsements from the hierarchy of organizations you have worked for upon your exit is probably worth more than any kind of monetary exit benefit you will receive. They are your guarantee of career continuity in a competitive job market and proof of your professional reputation.

Knowing not only how but *when* to either quit the game and leave the company is also key to ensure a respectful finish. There are circumstances when corporate dynamics are simply not favorable for you in that particular timing, or when prolonging your stay in a specific role / situation instead of beneficial might be damaging for your career or growth. For example, a boss that is not right in any way for you, minimal advancement opportunities, an unhealthy organizational culture or bad company reputation that might wear off your professional reputation, actually destroying your resume etc. These are all signs that you should be meticulously planning and preparing for your exit, but you get to choose when is the best timing for you to leave and organize your exit. You get to decide if waiting for the next paycheck, year-end bonus or any other important milestone (i.e. the boss of the above example is leaving) is worth more than an immediate exit.

THE ULTIMATE MOVE OF THE GAME: THE EXIT MOVE

Try to be constantly alert for shift in dynamics within the organization and be prepared to recognize that you might find yourself in a losing position or in a weak position.

Oftentimes a weak or losing position in the corporate game might not be at all a lack of talent or skill to play the game, given the complexity of the political game in most companies. You still and always have the power of choice on how deal with that and you always have the ultimate game move of planning your next step and your exit if required. If this is done in a conscious and planned fashion from you, it puts you back in a power position and you are still at the "top of your game", even though you made the choice to drop the game.

With an exit move you can reverse the former balance that might have not been favorable for you. By making a decision to exit the power balances reverses back to you. You still maintain your dignity, plus the endorsement and respect of the organization's leadership. Differently if you simply remain in this weak position without pursuing an exit move, you find yourself in a truly weak and losing position in the game. Being terminated from employment never looked well in anyone's career history regardless of reasonable justification. Always be in the position to dictate your ending of the game and if possible, also your terms. Don't let anyone show you the door. Try to be the one deciding when to walk out that door.

In conclusion, mastering the obscure rules of the game and understanding implicit power balances and dynamics not only will only prevent your downfall, but might actually prove as useful tools for advancing in corporate ladder apart from talent and skill, should you decide to practice carefully by them.

CHAPTER 3: CHECK YOUR NETWORK SETTINGS

Network;
Noun
A group or system of interconnected people.

Networks are important in many different parts of our lives. The importance of a strong business network inside or outside your organization therefore cannot be stressed enough.

Most people think of their business network at an operational level. That is the range of people with whom you are interacting with every day to get your operational tasks completed without any problems.

However, as it is described in the work of Linda Hill & Kent Lineback "Being the Boss: The 3 Imperatives for Becoming a Great Leader" (HBR Press, 2011), in order to be successful you need **not one, but three types of networks**: an operational network, a developmental network, and a strategic network.

Your developmental network is the collection of individuals whom you trust and to whom you can turn for advice. These are people who help you grow and develop professionally.

Your strategic network consists of individuals inside and outside of your organization whose position, experience and role will be able provide you with a future horizon and provoke your conventional view. This is the most difficult network to form because it is intentionally pursued from your side and can be difficult to neglect as you are absorbed by day to day operations.

Your "network settings" should include all of the above in order to secure success in the workplace.

WHERE ARE THE STRINGS ATTACHED

Apart from acknowledging and differentiating between your networks, one should also be aware of interconnections. There might be possible domino effects of your actions in a certain part of the organization if there are close yet seamless connection with another part you don't have in mind.

In your work environment just like any other environment, you should be investing some time to understand social networks and political interconnection. Even in a small family business of 10 people there are interconnections you should be aware of when working there and you should try to build solid foundations of your own amongst that network.

One might wonder, why identifying networks is such a important factor. Why would corporate networks be important if you are simply there to do your work – clock in – clock out and lead a simple nine to five lifestyle? The answer is fairly straightforward. It will at least keep you out of problems of any nature by making informed decisions and choices in the workplace first of all. So you can continue to lead your 9-5 lifestyle and maintain even your job security at least if not interested for anything more in terms of career advancement.

In any case knowing the networks and circles of influence within an organization, even if you are not part of them, will only provide you with opportunity.

INFLUENCING THROUGH NETWORKS

If you really master on the two above sections: having the 3 powerful types of networks & knowing the interconnections between networks in your organization, then you are ready to level up your game with the ultimate use of networking. This is no other than gaining influence through your networks!

This kind of indirect influencing through networks is a very powerful tool that fully complies with the two key principles of 'The Bow' as we mentioned in the previous chapter: Hierarchy & respect. You can only influence a network if you are in a position to recognize hierarchy and respect the key opinion leaders. The approach might seem simple in principle, but if you consider the complexity of modern-day Matrix structures and global organizations reporting lines and hierarchies become fuzzy and therefore recognizing and influencing networks can get truly complicated.

Influencing for sure isn't a quick fix. Expanding your circle of influence in a network and its interconnected networks requires mastery that comes only with conscious observation and practice. It can take time to develop empathy and awareness needed for effectively influencing others, but you are more likely to get what you want if you play a long game and are a truly reliable player.

The art of influencing doesn't come naturally to everyone. There are many sources of help and great business bibliography for you to develop your influencing skills and be at the top of your game.

THE KYF – KYE PRINCIPLES

There are two knowledge principles which are just as important in the workplace as they are in life:

KYF-knowing your friends

KYE-knowing your enemies

In any work scenario it is important to really know the difference between potential allies, 'friends' to those of neutral or hostile presence. In other words, you should always keep, at least mentally, a current and updated mapping of all the stakeholder you interact and impact with your work. Practice consciously in becoming more aware of other people's predispositions towards you and registering their networks and circles of influence.

This knowledge will provide an invaluable advantage for your, specifically when an adverse situation arises.

KYF: KNOW YOUR FRIENDS

Let's start with the 'knowing your friends' concept and immediately set the record straight by stating clearly that there are no true friendships in a business setting. There are people whose interests are best served by treating you amicably or by belonging in the same group in an organization and those you can call work 'friends.' These are usually your lunch break friends – those that you share your weekend hobbies update with, etc.

Always maintain a boundary of personal information you share at work with anyone and commit to not crossing that boundary ever and for no one. Being *friendly* with your colleagues is different to being friends. Being friendly is a must. Being friends is a major no.

My intention is not to be cynical about human relations and surely there are some rare exceptions, but I cannot stress enough the importance of being careful who you trust as your 'friend' in a work setting.

The higher up the career ladder you advance, the more "friends" you will discover that you suddenly have, trying to ensure any kind of benefit or preferential treatment that might be within your power. At that point you must be fair but firm, showing them that you have lines and boundaries that they as work colleagues must not cross.

At the same time, you need to nurture and constantly grow or maintain your network by remaining open and friendly towards others and letting them know that you are approachable, especially, if you are in a leadership position. Therefore, the KYF principle does not suggest to estranger yourself or isolate yourself from others. It is rather about knowing the level of trust and confidence you have towards the many people you connect with in your professional life. There is a big difference in being friend*ly* and a friend. KYF is just another concept of 'Corporate Karate' that you must master to stay at the top of the game.

KYE: KNOW YOUR ENEMIES

Keep your friends close, and your enemies closer as the famous saying goes. Surely knowing about potential opponents prevents you from "injuries" by preparing or avoiding interaction with them.

However, what I would suggest is not practicing a Machiavellian theory, but again stressing the fact how important it is to acknowledge not necessarily overt enemies but those even with potentially unfavorable predisposition towards you. These may even come at some stage from the above 'friendly' circle. It is actually most often that you experience negativity from the people that you have been closely collaborating with who are likely to be of neutral presence but will easily turn hostile if provoked.

In all circumstances with KYF and KYE, you must hold the knowledge of knowing your friends as well as knowing your enemies and act accordingly by being smart, thinking fast and always trying to be proactive in any given relationship within the workplace. You must be diplomatic between friend and foe yet proceed in a warrior-like approach to both to assure your success throughout the working environment.

CHAPTER 4 PLAYING THE GAME: MOVES, TACTICS, STRATEGY

Strategy;

Noun

The art and science of planning and marshalling resources for their most efficient and effective use. The term is derived from the Greek word for generalship or leading an army.

Tactics;

Means by which a strategy is carried out; planned and ad hoc activities meant to deal with the demands of the moment, and to move from one milestone to other in pursuit of the overall goal(s).

In the previous chapters we talked about learning the rules of the game and understanding the "players" in the corporate game (friends and enemies) and also the system they operate in, aka your network. Mastering this information, we are ready to move to the actual action setting of everyday corporate life.

It is very important to choose the correct approach concerning any situation within the workplace that may need different responsive tactical action depending on what/who you are dealing with in the company.

The thing that martial art athletes do instinctively is sizing up their opponent and deciding which fight tactic to use.

For our corporate karate game I would put these tactics in three big categories: passive defense, fight back or attack.

PASSIVE DEFENSE

Measures taken to reduce the probability of and to minimize the effects of damage caused by hostile action without the intention of taking the initiative.

It is a tactic that is translated to avoid taking any type of action from your side, aimed at minimizing damage. For example, in a situation where the power balance is not on your favor or you are unsure of the people you are dealing with, is best to keep a low profile. In a meeting for instance, it would be better to pass on the opportunity of either speaking up openly or in another situation making a decision to take action. I'm not suggesting that you remain inactive or that you miss the opportunity to show your competence or professional awareness and personal opinion, but to know when it is best to refrain from taking a stand. Play a more passive role in the situation until you get more information and you know how is best to act properly and how is best to proceed.

Be careful not to overuse this tactic, as it might come across to others as weakness. And nobody respects a weak player in a game!

ACTIVE DEFENSE/ FIGHT BACK

The employment of limited offensive action and counterattacks to deny a contested area or position to the enemy.

This tactic is deployed in the exact opposite case. In a situation that you feel confident you have all the information about and you know the power balance well within the corporate group, it makes sense that when you are being challenged or even attacked, in a sense, you need to fight back. Fighting back or defending your stand and your opinion whatever that situation might entail does not necessarily mean doing it with aggression.

Fighting back can be a simple response that would end any chance of a confrontation with the attacker and that response can be direct or as indirect as the one you have received that caused the issue because the simple fact that you are fighting back will usually end your attackers aggression towards the situation as the realization strikes that unless they are prepared for a corporate confrontation in the workplace it would be better for all concerned if they resolved the matter before the fight escalates.

ATTACK

This is a tactic that you are not responding to another's move, as the ones we covered before. You are on the contrary initiating the action directly upon or against a specific topic.

Attack in business terms would mean directly criticizing, disagreeing and challenging another person's opinion.

Attack of this kind is used in several instances & for different purposes:

1. One case is when confrontation cannot be avoided and in order to ensure success you only way is to actively move against someone or something standing in the way.

2. Another case is that attack is used as proactively defense mechanism. The well- known aphorism **"The best defense is a good offense"** that has been applied to many fields of endeavor, including games and military combat, is also very relevant and applicable to the business world. Here, the idea is a proactively strong offensive action, instead of a passive attitude will preoccupy the opposition and ultimately hinder its ability to mount an opposing counterattack, leading to a strategic advantage. Think about sales competition and who is able to make a move first to eliminate competition from a client with whatever offensive move is best applicable in that case.

3. **Attack** is also very commonly used **as a power display tactic** instead of results producing tactic like we described in the previous two cases. Especially from a level in the hierarchy and upwards, business meetings are less about what conclusion will be reached rather at whose voice will be heard over others and who will manage to appear superior. A high rank executive in a FTSE 100 company once shared with me his experiences of corporate meetings and told me that some are simply power demonstrations and for solving an issue between the corporate elite power-players in the company. The executive further added, that after a certain level, in order to be recognized and respected it is all about who you dare to confront and how you hold your own when you are in a meeting with other powerful corporate executives.

You can choose any of the tactics we describe fits best your purpose or circumstance. However, you should be consciously making a choice of tactic based on strategy not luck.

Aside of marketplace competition where attack is a straightforward necessity, offensive tactics are not to be used frequently as is not a healthy sign in an organization or person who uses this.

A workplace with frequent use or tolerance in offensive practices is a toxic environment that you most certainly need to leave from. If you find in such an environment you need to use any of the above tactics to survive there as long as you need to, but also immediately start planning your exit options and next move.

Even if attacks are not directed to you and you feel not impacted, this will not last for long. You are bound to find yourself in the middle of crossfire sooner or later in such an environment.

Below we will dedicate a section to recovering strategies and survival mechanisms when you find yourself in the middle of such situations.

CHAPTER 5: RECOVERING FROM SET-UPS & SET-BACKS - BUILDING RESILIENCE

Resilience;
Noun
The ability to be happy, successful, etc. again after something difficult or bad has happened

In the corporate environment you are certain to experience some form of set-ups and set-backs that you must quickly recover from in order to be successful. These set-ups and/or setbacks can seriously affect your progression up the corporate ladder and make your working life a daily struggle.

In reality resilience is adaptation in the face of adversity or stress in our case when workplace issues arise. The exciting thing about resilience is that it is a skill and like any skill, with practice, resilience can be learned.

Developing resilience skills is not only key to overcome difficulties but is also key to your success. Have you ever found yourself wondering what makes someone successful at work?

Chances are, like many people you imagine that the key to success at work is intelligence or going above and beyond the demands of the role such as working long hours or taking on extra commitments. However, in modern workplaces characterized by staff cutbacks, deadlines, rivalry and organizational change, success relies on an individual's capacity to cope and even thrive when faced with stress.

Resilient employees build strong **connections and relationships** with others (Davis Laak, 2014). These high-quality relationships can be characterized by a number of features. Connections are characterized by effective communication in which an individual listens actively and is responsive to their colleague and their emotions (Davis Laak, 2014). In positive workplace relationships, a resilient worker will do what they can to help another person to achieve success in the workplace. The resilient worker is a team-player who aims for a win-win with their fellow employees and is happy to see them progress, without demonstrating any negatively competitive attitude towards them.

Next resiliency mechanism is the networking we analyzed previously. Social support plays an important role in workplace resilience (Jackson, Firtko, & Edenborough, 2007). It is beneficial to develop personal as well as professional **networks**, which can be a source of guidance and support during times of stress or simply to provide a nurturing relationship. It is also helpful for employees to have contact with colleagues outside of their own immediate work setting. These people can provide validation to the worker and can potentially be accessible to the individual when accessing support within their own work situation would make the employee vulnerable (Jackson et al., 2007).

Modern workplaces are certainly typified by stress. Technology and access to the Internet mean that, for many, work is a constant presence. No longer does one establish a career which they then stay in for the duration of their working life. Resilient employees are able to manage stress effectively so it is not overwhelming and detrimental (Davis Laak, 2014). By actively engaging in **self-care** and nurturing themselves after a stressful incident, however minor, resilient employees avoid 'burnout'.

Finally, employees with resiliency tend to show "grit". Grit is that **fighting spirit** that sets some employees apart. It can be defined as 'having the passion and perseverance to pursue your long-term goals' (Davis Laak, 2014). Whoever has that passion to strive for achieving challenging goals, this will almost certainly mean that they will encounter obstacles. Therefore, when this occurs, workers have the chance to build resilience, as resilience is needed to overcome these hurdles and set- backs.

CHAPTER 6: THE HUNGER FOR POWER GAMES

Power;
Noun
The capacity or ability to direct or influence the behavior of others or the course of events

Power has very commonly a negative association, not unjustifiably maybe, but I would dare say misleadingly. Think the opposite of power, which is no other than powerlessness. Being in a weak position to express one's opinion or exercise their options is surely not a positive thing at all and most certainly it worse than being in a position of power. There is nothing dark or wrong with power itself, but rather the way you use it and the kind of "games" you play using power. In the corporate game where the natural environment within which people interact is a hierarchical and complex ecosystem, power games are very common.

In their classic study of power, that social psychologists John R. P. French and Bertram H. Raven conducted in 1959, they stated that power is divided into five separate and different forms: Coercive Power, Reward Power, Legitimate Power, Referent Power & Expert Power.

Depending on what type of power is being used (or misused), political games fall exactly into the above five power categories. However, one common thing among all types of Power Games is that they are designed to give the player some type of advantage over others.

Players of power games players are either trying to increase the level of their power or demonstrate the power they already have. Some players have truly dire intentions. Others are merely self-centered, and in this case their game can be named as ego-game too.

LEGITIMATE OR TITULAR POWER

This is the power that comes from one's role or title in the corporate hierarchy, therefore also very commonly referred to as titular power. By default, a Manager has less titular power than a Director and respectively a Director less than a VP. This means of course ultimate decision-making authority and forcing others to act in a certain way due to one's superior authority.

Very common power games associated with this type of power are the pleasing of the powerful game & the control game.

In the pleasing game, players are the employees who tend to overwhelm their powerful targets with compliments & fake appreciation of their opinions, never openly disagreeing with them. The gain obviously for them if the favorable opinion of the power holders for them and the respective direct or indirect benefits they receive from it.

In the control game, the payoff for the players is the domination over others. The players in this case are usually supervisors, managers and generally people with titular power. People with titular power can completely control others at work leaving no room for personal expression or freedom to others in their tasks.

Titular power in reality is a very weak form of power. It lasts as long as the tile stays with the person and disappears immediately after the person no longer holds that role!

COERCIVE & REWARD POWER

Coercive and reward power are two sides of the same coin. The first comes from the ability to impose sanctions or punishments to avoid undesired actions or behavior and the other from rewarding specific action or behavior that lead to desired results. Like titular power, rewards and punishments only go so far. One of the main limitations of these types of power is that they are very extrinsic. Extrinsic motivation does work in the short term, but it just doesn't inspire people or changes really their behavior.

One can choose to play the punishment card and will get a guaranteed enemy from it. As soon as the power dynamic changes this player will have to face the consequences. Also the player that chooses the reward game is in for a loss. Soon the reward needed to attain the same result or behavior will need to become bigger and then it might even become to high a price to be able to afford it.

REFERENT POWER

This is nothing less than popularity and being really well liked by others in your organization. Of course, this can imply lots of charisma or beauty or politeness or any trait in general that can make someone popular with their co-workers in the organization. An example of a player with referent power is an employee who is very popular and likeable by his co-workers, however not performing well in his job. Being likeable the right people and in the right networks as we discussed above provides you with opportunity and leverage. Also, the "Halo Effect" of the personal popularity can either conceal shortcomings allowing low effort and high gain.

Let's take an example of a weak manager with only titular power and low referent power of their own who has a not well performing employee with high referent power. This manager might never take the "risk" of the unpopular decision of terminating someone liked by many as this will make them look bad and will deteriorate their unpopularity. Such a player (the manager) would be valuing more their own game than respecting and protecting the organization they work for.

Finally, similar to the referent power is another concept known as connections power. We have already discussed about the power and use of networks in a previous chapter. This type of power does not have to do with your title and hierarchical position in an organization. It comes purely from who you know in the organization. A common example of connections power is the case of a promotion. Among internal candidates for a promotion it is not necessarily the one with the best performance or skills that will get promoted, but the one that receives the most votes of trust by the senior management. The deciding factor becomes then how good the person is ***perceived*** to be, regardless of their true value to the organization or quality of work.

EXPERT OR INFORMATIONAL POWER

Expert power is related to one's unique skillset and abilities compared to others in the organization. Rare skills are highly paid and retained at all costs by organizations.

Types of expertise range from very deeply specialized and sophisticated skills or very simple ones, which however are vital for business continuity in an organization. An example of a modest skill that however makes one an indispensable expert in their organization could merely the knowledge of operation of a specific software (usually an outdated or overly customized one, that nobody else knows in the market and the company itself). Or being the single owner of a unique task in the organization having solely all necessary information to complete that type of work.

In the above examples, the employees who hold the expert power have an advantageous position in this power game Vs. their management and organization. If they are also aware of the power they hold and are not willing to play fair, this ends usually in a problematic way for everyone.

Another very common power game that people play with expert power is holding back information and not sharing knowledge. This type of player is usually a tenured employee who deliberately is not willing to share with a newly hired colleague any knowledge and information around his area of expertise, task or the organization itself.

Withholding purposefully information and controlling the flow of information shared with their team is a very common example of "old school" managers who feel in power by keeping their teams in the dark. Usually this kind of game is played by insecure profiles who as people managers fail to delegate work. Their direct reports experience a robot like, meaningless task orientated daily work routine and eventually feel disengaged from the organization and most likely quit.

CHAPTER 7: GAME OVER

The concept of "job for life" with which the Baby Boomer generation was brought up has long ceased to exist. Today's workforce across the globe knows that will have to change an average of five times at least their career within their lifetime. The millennial generation of workers are projected to take up 75% of the workforce by 2025, while meta-millennials are already entering the global workforce as these lines are being written. And without wanting to repeat tons of conclusions written on these generations' characteristics, I will only say that nor a typical job, neither a single one employer will satisfy the aspirations and lifestyle of our "digital native" workforce!

As a result, leaving a job or an employer and exiting from any corporate game is not an unlikely scenario or a concept left for the day of retirement, many years away from today. Exiting the game is something you need to be aware and keep in mind all the time while you are still "in the game". The same way you make careful planning on how to enter the corporate game, how to keep yourself *in* the game, you also need to have a plan on how and when to exit the game, exactly as we talked about in Chapter 2 in the respectful finish and ultimate move rule.

Before deciding for any game that it is over, apart from personal career planning considerations and priorities, make sure you reach out to your developmental network that we discussed before and sense check all factors leading to your decision and that your exit move is for the better.

In case however the decision that the corporate game is over is not a voluntary one, but is announced to you expectedly or unexpectedly, then I would advise that you don't try to negotiate the exit itself but rather anything around its terms.

The good news is that even if corporate game is over you for any kind of reason, even the most unimaginable one to you, like the company you work for collapses and declares suddenly one day bankruptcy, as happened with the case of Thomas Cook after 178 year of operation, or if your position is simply being restructured, life still goes on.

And life is the most spectacular game on earth.

CHAPTER 8: EPILOGUE

Supernova;
A supernova is the explosion of a star.

Having too much matter causes the star to explode, resulting in a
supernova.
A supernova occurs at the end of a single star's lifetime.

I'm going to be somewhat too poetic for a business book context, referring to my two favorite scientific fields, astronomy and history.

Every beginning has an ending. And every ending is a new beginning.

It's a law of nature that nothing lasts forever.

This law applies the same way, whether we are talking about a supernova in our galaxy that has reached the end of its galactic existence and is about to transform to a huge explosion gifting us with amazing colors and formations to observe; or about the ending of magnificent empires of the ancient world like the Persian or Egyptian dynasties, that held in their hands all the power of the known world at the time, but eventually succumbed to defeat by new power dynamics.

Your corporate game is a part of life. Of your valuable and limited time on this earth.

So, use your time wisely.

Try to not get carried away by the fierce of battle and try to be fair while playing the game.

Regularly check your inner self. Do not let the game change your core values and always remember who you are as a person.

Try to shine like a star during your game. Not only by excelling in your results, but also by shedding only your light to others around you, and avoiding to shed any toxic dust that all stars have in their system.

And when it's time to conclude your game round, leave the game like a supernova.

Leave behind your "stellar formation" and light. Leave behind your example, so that younger generations can observe, be marveled by and learn from.

Be a supernova: extremely bright and super-powerful.

(*) P.S. you might want to avoid the blast and explosion as a supernova when you are in the game!

ABOUT THE AUTHOR

Angelina Michail is the country Head of Human Resources for a global company. With more than 15 years of corporate experience, her own business start-up and academically teaching H.R.M., Angelina has always been passionate about sharing knowledge that can improve others. "Corporate Karate: martial arts in business suits", is her first book, but she has been a regular article contributor to various business publications since 2005, both in print and online.

She holds a Ba in Philosophy, Education & Psychology (majoring in Psychology) from Ioannina University in Greece and an MSc in Human Resources Management from Cardiff Business School, UK (Dissertation awarded with distinction 80%).

When not making a business impact in her organization or writing books, Angelina can be found travelling across unconventional parts of our planet, exploring new coffee tastes in her hometown Athens, Greece or jogging with her Beagle puppy, Milly. Milly is already a big fan of Angelina's book, especially the "edible" print version of it!

AKNOWLEDGEMENTS

This book has a long history from its inception to the publish stage. It has been written in different phases the past couple of years between a demanding corporate and travelling life plus moving houses and raising a puppy! So, despite many reasons to let it go, I always had a supportive bunch by my side to urge me to continue.

Big thanks to my family: mommy Katerina for unfailingly following up my publication date, dad Tasos for just being dad I guess, and looking impressed with whatever I do, my sister Anastasia for always reassuring me we'll get there and for always providing the IT and Web solution of everything, Ioanna my youngest sister Ioanna for being the creative spirit behind and of course Milly's best friend.

Big thanks to my dear friends: Yiota, Panagiotis and Irini for supporting me all these years with their friendship and care, and for being a great company to drink wine and eat Italian food after each drama! **Big thanks also to:** my teacher Gail for being the reason I've loved writing in English since I was five years old. Linda for being more than a great manager and debunking the myth that everyone in corporate is cold and indifferent. Theodore for trusting me first time with leading a team when I was 28.